THREE WORDS
THAT SHOULD ROCK YOUR WORLD

A DEVOTIONAL

CHERYL A. DURHAM, PH.D.

Cover Art: When the senses are shaken – Intaglio colour etching by William Blake from his 1796 book 'A Large Book of Designs'
From: commons.wikimedia.org

Copyright © 2013 Cheryl Durham

All rights reserved.

ISBN-13: 978-1495964817
ISBN-10: 1495964817

TABLE OF CONTENTS

CHAPTER 1 - INTRODUCTION 1

CHAPTER 2 - INQUIRY 7

CHAPTER 3 - INQUIRY: WEEK ONE 17

CHAPTER 4 - INQUIRY: WEEK TWO 21

CHAPTER 5 - INQUIRY: WEEK THREE 25

CHAPTER 6 - INQUIRY: WEEK FOUR 31

CHAPTER 7 –INTEGRATION: WRESTLING WITH MY PARADIGM 35

CHAPTER 8 - IMPLEMENTING CHANGE 41

CHAPTER 8 - CONCLUDING THOUGHTS 45

CHAPTER 9 - RESOURCES 51

ABOUT THE AUTHOR 57

CHAPTER 1 - INTRODUCTION

If you grew up as a Christian, when you hear these three words you may not be alarmed immediately; however, the paradigm that you have been taught to use when reading the Bible and interpreting its meaning is most likely NOT the paradigm that the writers of the New Testament, or even the Old Testament used.

While even this may not shock you, what you do not understand is that it should. Our Western way of thinking and knowing and interpreting our world is so different from that of the 1st Century believing community. However, what is more amazing is that we do not even notice. When we read the Bible, we often assume that when Jesus came to establish something called the Church and that Paul, after having his 'experience' with Jesus on the road to Damascus, converted to Christianity. Paul apparently then realized that the reason Jesus came was to get rid of the Jewish system of religion, and to start a new one called Christianity. This is a myth.

Despite the fact that not one of these things is true, we go on believing them anyway. Why is that? How can we believe that Jesus, Paul, and the other Apostles thought and acted the way the Church does today? Their religious practice looked nothing like today's Christian Church religious practice no matter what the type – Catholic, Protestant, or Evangelical.

We tend to think that the religious experience of the New Testament writers and Jesus matched our view of reality today. It is as though we have completely rewritten the historical record. Have we? I believe that we have, and I believe that the historical record bears this out.

Step outside what you know to be true for a moment; you are free to pick it up again after you investigate what I am saying. Take everything you think you know about Jesus and just set it down for a moment. Listen carefully; are you ready? The three words that should rock your world are these; **Jesus is Jewish!**

If your brain does not start firing off questions when you read this, there might be a problem. Please email me if this is the case. This study is on the implications of that statement.

You can get a free study every month if you are a member of the Living Truth Network. Please go to livingtruthnetwork.com to sign up.

Enjoy! I hope you have had time to think about those words. In the coming weeks we will discuss much more.

Shalom,

Cheryl

Three Words That Should Rock Your World

CHAPTER 2 - INQUIRY

Did Jesus have a cell phone, and if not, can I put one in his hand?

Simple Answer: Jesus did not have a cell phone, and you cannot put one in His hand unless you are trying to tell Him who He is.

This may seem like a ridiculous question at first, but it has a direct correlation with the way we often impose anachronism (the representation of an event, person, or thing in a historical context in which it could not have occurred or existed) on our scripture. Why are some things obvious and other things almost invisible, even though they are right in front of us?

People say many things that they assume to be true, either mistakenly or out of ignorance, when they are not. In most cases, when challenged, people do not respond well to criticism. This is problematic, especially when it comes to spiritual growth. If one is always growing, there will always be something to learn. That learning doesn't come through a direct personal voice from God as many are led to believe. It comes from members of the community, the human one. What happens when we insist on believing and promoting what may not be true?

Unfortunately, there are many people who, when shown the truth of a matter, insist on believing what they want to believe despite the fact that there is significant evidence to the contrary. Even worse, many of these people are Christians who would rather believe a lie than to uphold the actual teachings of Jesus and the Apostle Paul in the New Testament witness. The term for this could be 'worldview' worship or in other words, MY view is more important than that of Jesus.

My question is directed toward a person who rejects factual information about Jesus. Is he or she truly a "believer" in Christ or is he or she rather a believer in something quite different? What is a Christian anyway?

If Jesus identified solely with the Jewish community, which He did, and followed a Second Temple Jewish religion completely throughout his life, then why would someone claiming to be His follower do something different? If Jesus walked the Earth today, would He still be a Jew? Of Course! So where would he find his community? With Christians? (Think that through).

In Jesus' world, there was no such thing as an individual (that's a Greek philosophical one and not a Second Temple Hebrew one). Jesus came to bring in the Kingdom of God and to inaugurate it through His death and resurrection. He came to establish, not to do away with Torah as the way to live with God.

So, two particular issues stand out for me, as I hear them all the time. The first one is the idea that "individual salvation" and "individual freedom" come from the Bible, and the second is that the "new" covenant eliminated the need of God's people to be Torah observant. Neither of these two ideas is Biblical. There are many more of these ideas, but not enough room in this document to discuss. New studies will come out each month.

Jesus never preached that, nor did His followers. This begs the question as to where do we get these ideas? What worldview incorporates these ideas? These ideas could be the 'cell phone' that we cannot put in His hand.

These Christian ideas developed over a hundred years after Jesus and Paul left the Earth by people who took incredible creative license without any authority to do it.[1]

Yet, Christians still act as though the historical facts about Jesus and the NT writers did not exist. Or worse yet they believe that these ideas came directly from the pages of Scripture.

We laugh at the idea of Jesus with a cell phone, but really have no clue about, and continue to use anachronisms that are not products of our contemporary age and worldview. Has anyone thought that if they saw Jesus on the street

---

[1] See Dacy, and Soulen among many others

and called out the name "Jesus", He would keep on walking? Why? Because it wasn't His name! We assume that the first century community (because there was NO CHURCH) is just like the church down the street. That assumption could not be farther from the truth.

It is imperative that Christians become knowledgeable about Christian history as it relates to the Jewish religion of Jesus and the Apostles as the validity of Christianity as a religion is uncertain. We do not have the "individual freedom" to do whatever we want with no consequences to the rest of the body, Jew and Gentile, who by the way are not separate religious bodies. Christian ignorance keeps Jesus from returning. He is waiting for us to act. When we do what HE already told us to do, but we ignore, then perhaps He'll return. Hopefully He will not decide enough is enough, and bring judgment. I believe Jonathan Edwards sermon "Sinners in the Hands of an Angry God" might apply here.

Feigned ignorance due to complacency on our parts will not rescue us from whatever consequences result in a falling away from God. Therefore, if you are a Christian, and you do not know Jesus' real name, real religion, and real mission, I would start looking. You never know when there might be a pop quiz.

Work on one verse a week. Read these verses and answer the questions. If you come up with more questions than answers GOOD!

Write them in the notes section so you can research them. Look up the links and reference materials and take notes on what you learn.

CHAPTER 3 - INQUIRY: WEEK ONE

Verse: Matthew 16:18-20

"Upon this rock I will build my ekklesia...Whatever you bind on earth will be bound in heaven"

Yeshua did not start 'the Church'

Keep in mind that the word 'church' was not added to the bible until the 17th Century (around 1611) at the insistence of England's King James (after whom the KJV is named) to insert the word 'church' where the words assembly or congregation occurred. This was specifically to secure his own power over the people. See rule #3.[2] The King James Version of the Bible is the 'official' version because King James was the King, and he held the power to make that happen.

There were several words from the Septuagint (LXX) that were used to describe the gathering of believers. These would include:

---

[2] see also ekklesia in Resource Section

- ekklesia (called out, assembly convened for deliberating, town council)

- eydah (assembled by appointment, with a purpose, congregations)

- k'hilah (assembly, convocation, congregations, assembly for war or invasion, for religious purposes, feasts, worship, company, multitude)

- synagogee (community, gathered, assembly) (Gorelik *Antisemitism* 10)

But 'church' was not among them.

Week One Questions:

1. If Yeshua was not talking about 'church' but rather an assembly of believers, why change it?

2. If Yeshua had something else in mind, why is that not taught?

3. If the text does not read 'Church', could translation be a problem?

4. Does seeing Yeshua within His Second-Temple Jewish context change the meaning?

5. Do you wonder why you did not already know this?

6. Why do you think the church does not teach this meaning?

CHAPTER 4 - INQUIRY: WEEK TWO

Yeshua practiced Judaism not Christianity

<u>Verse:</u> **Exodus 12:1-28 and Luke 22:7-20 (especially 14-20)**

"Do <u>this</u> in remembrance of Me"

We can see in the above verses that Yeshua not only identified with the community of Israel, but He was also strictly Torah-observant and taught His disciples to observe the feasts. The 'cup' that He took with them is the part of the meal known as the *'meal of the Messiah'* in the Passover celebration. It is the last cup of wine and one does not eat afterwards. Yeshua's act was not one of starting a new religion called Christianity. It was the perfect act of religious observance of a Second-Temple Jew. This interpretation clashes with the idea of 'Eucharist' and communal meal not connected with Passover.

Week Two Questions:

1. Does your 'church' celebrate Passover as Yeshua did with His disciples? Why or why not?

2. Why is this context missing from the church's history?

3. If in the Exodus passage we see that God has given this as a perpetual (meaning forever) celebration, why don't we do it?

4. Yeshua's comment about "fulfilled" in verse 16 means established forever. How does this conflict with your view?

5. If Yeshua was fully Torah observant, as we see in these two passages, how can we say he abolished the Law?

6. Are you beginning to see some inconsistencies within the Christian paradigm? Where? What?

CHAPTER 5 - INQUIRY: WEEK THREE

Verse: Matthew 28:18-20

And Jesus came up and spoke to them saying, "All authority has been given to Me in heaven and on earth. Go Therefore and make disciples of all the nations, baptizing them in the name of the Father and the Son and the Holy Spirit, teaching them to observe all that I commanded you; and lo, I am with you always, even to the end of the age."

Jesus taught others to make Jews out of Gentiles, not Christians out of Jews.

In this verse, Yeshua is telling his Jewish disciples to continue His ministry. He gives them the authority out of the Authority that God give Him, which is 'all authority in heaven and earth'.

The word 'go' does not mean to 'go' somewhere; it should be translated, 'while you are going', or in other words, 'as you are living your life...' The words "*all nations*" are an idiomatic expression for Gentiles or non-Jews. This has a huge impact on some current evangelical thought on who is evangelizing whom.

Verse 19, "Go therefore..." is often used as a "formula" for use in baptism; however, there is historical evidence that this verse does not even exist in any manuscript dated earlier than the Byzantine text of Constantine.[3]

Disciples were making *Jews out of Gentiles* not *Christians out of Jews.* All the first-century believers, even Paul's converts, thought of themselves as Jews. They did not see themselves as 'Christians'. So where is the Church?

---

[3] See David King's comments after Skip Moen's Article, www.SkipMoen.com, "http://skipmoen.com/2013/09/04/matthew-2819-from-a-bible-of-1568/

Week Three Questions:

1. What is He telling His Jewish disciples about His authority?
2. 2. What is He telling them to teach?
3. 3. What does Yeshua mean by teaching them to observe all that I have taught you to do?
4. 4. Can you see that Yeshua is telling his disciples to teach Torah observance (see above)?
5. 5. Can you see that this is not an evangelical message

that is compatible with 21st-century Christian evangelical ideas?
6. 6. Why not?

Three Words That Should Rock Your World

Chapter 6 - Inquiry: Week Four

Verse: Matthew 5:18

For truly I say to you, until heaven and earth pass away, not the smallest letter or stroke shall pass from the Law until all is accomplished.

Jesus upheld the Torah because He was Jewish.

He did not do away with it for Christianity; rather, He established it for His community Israel. Since *not all* things are fulfilled, (established) Torah is in full effect for believers today.

In this verse, Yeshua establishes Torah; He is not abolishing it. Some in the Christian world see the idea of Law from a Greek perspective. A Greek idea of Law limits, however, the LAW from a Hebraic view is freedom (see resources for more information). God has established Torah as His instructions for a relationship with Him. Can we object to that?

Questions:

1. If Yeshua is establishing Torah until He returns or later, then how is it possible that He is also saying one does not have to follow it?

2. What is Yeshua's view? Is He a Greek or a Hebrew?

3. If Yeshua is a Torah-obedient Israelite, then why would he tell others not to follow?

4. Do you see now that to believe that Yeshua abolished Torah is to abolish Yeshua as well?

5. What things have you learned from this verse?

Three Words That Should Rock Your World

CHAPTER 7 – INTEGRATION: WRESTLING WITH MY PARADIGM

If you have thought about Jesus or Yeshua (which is His real name), you may have concluded that the things you have previously understood about Him may have been incorrect or misinterpreted.

We have seen that making Him a Christian is like putting a cell phone in His hand. This is an historical fallacy called anachronism. While we would laugh to think Yeshua 'texted'

Peter, we do not seem to get the same chuckle from calling his community the Church.

We have learned that throughout the last two millennia, there have been translators who may have had agendas other than *accurate* transmission of the text.

We have learned that much misinformation has been spread because of ignorance, and because of that misinformation, mistakes are made in translation, teaching, and preaching of the text.

In the next study guide, think about how this has affected your thinking. Keep in mind that your 'experience of God' will not change. It is only in the interpretation or the 'meaning' of the text. It is only the meaning of that experience that must change in order to say that you are a follower of the Word or a follower of Yeshua.

Questions:

In the following sections, write your thoughts and questions.

Anachronisms are things that do not fit the setting of the text. For example a cell phone in Yeshua's hand. What other anachronisms come to mind when thinking about

Yeshua's time and the things people say about Him?

What misinterpretations, misinformation, or mistakes do you think about now that you recognize that Yeshua was not putting Torah (the Law) away?

Personal Reflection:

How does this affect my thinking about God?

How do I think about Jesus now? Who is He?

How do I think about the things Jesus says? Have they been 'Christianized'?

What does God think about what the Church has done with His covenant/people?

Should all this knowledge influence my walk?

CHAPTER 8 - IMPLEMENTING CHANGE

Gained knowledge is only helpful when we implement change.

As a result of what you learned this month think about the following things, and what you will do with what you learned!

How should this make an impact on my walk?

What needs to change?

What does that look like?

Conclusion

More questions: Learning always creates more questions. Write them here so that you can come back to them later.

1.

2.

3.

4.

Three Words That Should Rock Your World

CHAPTER 8 - CONCLUDING THOUGHTS

Simply Share what you have learned~

What Have I Learned about Jesus as a Jew? How do I see Him now?

_____
_____
_____
_____
_____
_____

Three Words That Should Rock Your World

Three Words That Should Rock Your World

Three Words That Should Rock Your World

Three Words That Should Rock Your World

_____

_____

_____

_____

_____

_____

_____

_____

_____

_____

_____

Three Words That Should Rock Your World

CHAPTER 9 - RESOURCES

Books

Levine, Amy-Jill, Dale C. Allison, and John Dominic. Crossan. *The Historical Jesus in Context*. Princeton: Princeton UP, 2006. E-book, Kindle.

Levine, Amy Jill. "Misusing Jesus: How the Church Divorces Jesus from Judaism." *Christian Century,* Dec 26 (2006): 20-25. Print.

Soulen, R. Kendall. *The God of Israel and Christian Theology*. Minneapolis: Fortress,1996. Print.

Williamson, Clark M., *A Guest in the House of Israel: Post-Holocaust Church Theology*. Louisville: Westminster/John Knox, 1993. Print.

Videos

http://www.youtube.com/watch?v=LjAWyg7ZCJk

http://www.youtube.com/watch?v=VuVUO-xUdrQ

Websites

Skip Moen's Today's Word

http://skipmoen.com/

Frontline Video about the Historical Jesus

http://www.pbs.org/wgbh/pages/frontline/shows/religion/jesus/bornliveddied.html

Scholars to watch:

Skip Moen

Bob Gorelik

Brad Young

Daniel Boyarin

Pamela Eisenbaum

John Gager

Lloyd Gaston

Ken Soulen

David Flusser

Mark Nanos

Ideas to investigate:

King James' rules for translation:

http://www.kjvonly.org/other/kj_instructs.htm

The word *Ekklesia*-

http://skipmoen.com/2014/01/14/flash-mob/

The Name of Jesus:

http://www.youtube.com/watch?v=VZtWlmjH35w

Three Words That Should Rock Your World

ABOUT THE AUTHOR

Cheryl is a wife, mother, grandmother, entrepreneur and author. She has been a Biblical Facilitator since 1996, and is currently on the Board of Trustees of Living Truth serving as Board Liaison to Ministries. You can contact Cheryl by email: Cheryl@livingtruth.us

She has a Master's degree in Biblical Counseling, and a Doctor of Biblical Studies in Contemporary Apologetics and Theology and a Ph.D. in Judeo-Christian Theology under the direction of Skip Moen from the Master's Theological Research Institute where she is also on staff. Her website and virtual classroom can be found at www.livingtruthnetwork.com where Biblical Facilitators and distance learning students can find resources and encouragement.